A PANDEMIC POETRY, COVID-19

CHARLES MWEWA

Africa in Canada Press
Ottawa, Canada, 2021

DEDICATION

To all those who are infected, affected or have
survived the fangs of Covid-19 virus; to all those
who have succumbed and died from its lethal sting.
To you all, this little book is dedicated.

CONTENTS

PREFACE

The coronavirus (Covid-19) pandemic has devastated the people of the world. Within a span of one year (between March 2020 and March 2021) about 112 million people contracted the virus, with approximately 2.5 million deaths from the virus. Life as the world knew it came to a stand-still – masks replaced facial make-ups, and social distancing became a new social routine. Nations and cities closed, so were companies and businesses. Those who worked in the healthcare corridors became essential workers, and the common flu took a back role in surrender to Covid-19. Scheduled agendas and activities got cancelled, and remote learning and trading became a norm.

Families were separated, and companies of friends and loved ones were proscribed. In one year, some people experienced the reverse of fortunes, while others took advantage of the pandemic and enriched themselves. The vaccine gave some temporary hope to the world, until the virus morphed and took on newer and more complex variances. It was a race against time; it was hope against hope.

These poems bring the vagaries of the time to note and provide the hope for tomorrow. I would like to acknowledge my two daughters, Emmerance and Tashany-Idyllia, who, in the absence of their mother (who went to another city for work) remained with me and assisted in the chores at home so I could find time to write. I am mostly indebted to the two for their hard work and care in tending to their youngest sibling, Cuteravive.

Charles Mwewa
Ottawa, 2021

1. Down Corona Lane

Down the Lane named Corona, lives a virus
It has been gloomily, untimely brought upon
us
Down the Lane of Corona, sounds are
muted
All routine adventures have been civilly re-
routed
There is rarely a person walking,
Neither is there a muse talking
All is quiet, deathly silent, as if life had ended
The way of normalcy, prematurely
suspended
Fear proudly prowls an empty street in
disguise
And staying at home is seen as damagely
wise
Heaven and Hell receive more souls
Forever shunting them in eternal thralls
Under the shadow of Corona families thrive
There is more cash on which to sparkly
survive
Mobility is a race from room to room, out is
rare,
But herein, the art of complete manuscript is
there.
Down Corona Lane, same is gone
Down Corona Lane, game is done.

2. Los Angeles

Thou art magnificent, O thou city with
Angeles
Thou hath no equivalent, serve Domini
Angelus
Thy mountainous Bel Air, thy flattened
Beverley
Hills
Indeed, thy hilly Hollywood, thy unseen
Hidden
Hills,
These brilliances in their eternally glorious
Calabasas
Wouldst Orange County volitionally be
"Birth of Jesus"?
Down thy lively lit boulevards mine sweetie
droveth
Up at thy vetted Disneyworld, mine little
angels roveth
In thy lux hotels, dreams of effulgence
hugeth mine soul
In thy fabulous indulgence, mine senses
fluently roll
Oh City, a place whereth I would again
rather be,
After Covid-19, O City, me orisoneth
rebound thee.

3. I Can't Breathe

"I can't breathe," three words, three last
words
Words that have ruined lives, damaged
worlds
Oh, Minneapolis, don't you hear him, dying?
His chocked head, cop's knee on his neck,
frying?
The indictment, because George Floyd is
black?
He didn't walk free, he woke up, all was dark
Oh, cry you all who hate, hate and love, love
Even Eric Garner, his eleven calls, quake
above
There is a war raging, xenophobia is the bate
Should looking different be judgmental fate?
Don't tell me White people are racists, nope
I know many noble Whites, many preach
hope
Oh hatred, O Covid-19, you're ruthless
killers
You're cowards, you feast on and butcher
pillars,
You, ruthless homophobes, you, brutal
tribalists,
You're heartless, you're fake, damned
nihilists
You target the weak, helpless, you cause
misery

Your hearts are deadly, your anger is blistery,
Oh, deny, deny them power and authority,
For they abuse it, wrathing it on the
minority.

4. America

America, America, Oh, America, the great
Founded on stolen estate and historical hate
Oh, land, developed by injustice of slave
labor
And invigorated by angst one against
neighbor
Your soldiers to foreign countries do harm
Saddam and Ghaddafi, you murdered by
firearm
But George Floyd, you slaughtered, wrong
Your streets do riot, violence you now
prolong
For your president, Trump, knows no clue
His style of leadership, tenders a racist skew
Oh America, your wealth, rests on Black
sweat
Surely, you've weaponized race, with no stet.
Your bigoted police him killed in broad day-
light
Your towns lit with gory, nights fill with
blight.

5. Pandemic of Racism, I

Declare it all,
say it all,
write it all,
record it all.
My people,
African people,
all over the world,
have been victims
of a pandemic called racism
The characteristics of which are obvious,
namely:
Character is secondary,
the hate monster reigns;
Intellect is third,
the evil of hatred drives agendas;
Love of danger is fourth,
all Blacks are suspects;
And cruelty is last,
Africans must be punished.
From the shores
of Benguanaland,
cries rise,
A mother has just lost a son,
taken by slavers.
A wife is now windowed,
though husband's alive.
And children will grow up
without two parents.

In haciendas of America,
backs reel with pain,
Masters spoil Black thighs,
with no alimony given.
Men and boys
toil endless fields,
with no pay.

6. Pandemic of Racism, II

New immigrants
drive dyeing industrial cranes.
"I can't breathe, my face is gone, please"
falls in death eyes,
this Black man must die.
Oh, Mother,
Oh, my late father,
did you know,
that chickens are killed
with ample dignity,
that animals
have rights activities for them to advocate?
And Derek Chauvin
is charged with third degree.
And is immediately free
on a million dollars bond.
I ask: Where did he get such
with a police officer's salary?
Oh, how unheard of,
for such brutal killing?
An African
would have been lamped with first,
He would have been assigned
death penalty.
And he would have been
gazetted a "demon."

7. Pandemic of Racism, III

Africa,
Africans,
Africans descent nationals,
why have you paid so much,
just for being black?
For over four hundred years,
you've agonized.
For many centuries,
you've been abused.
You've overtly been disregarded
as humans;
Not so long ago,
you were things,
property even.
Not so many years long,
you were flogged.
And not so long ago,
your continent was stolen,
your young healthy ones captured,
taken away.
Your old folks,
beaten,
stricken,
slain
murdered
butchered.
And your hallowed African cultures,
forsaken.

Oh, haters of Blacks,
stop,
cease,
end
terminate;
you aren't
feared
you aren't
not jeered.

8. They Count

They called you floor sweeper,
a toilet cleaner
They did not invite you
to make TV talk
When they gathered
and made future plans
You were deliberately forgotten,
useless
They make you hate your profession,
shameful
At college and university,
you were dung,
least
You were paid less,
working conditions,
worse
You feared to introduce yourself,
you're embarrassed
You became a nurse,
because you couldn't be a doctor
You cleaned people's shit,
and they despised you.
oh, janitor,
oh, grocery seller,
oh, fuel pumper.
No-one loved you,
everybody hated you,
for null
They said,

"You're not an engineer, you're a
technician."
They compared you
to a lost cause.
But hypocrites them they celebrated,
ululated.
They called them stars,
paid them billions.
But you are only living
pay-to-pay,
near poverty.
Where are movie stars,
soccer players,
NBA,
NHL?
Where are
"Big Bosses,"
"Big Bishops"
or MLB?
Where are
bright lawyers,
smart judges,
or the showstoppers?
Where are
professors,
airline pilots
or money-managers?
With their big bucks,
they have disappeared,
gone.
Oh, see, a farmer,
made me see another day,

today.
Underpaid mail-delivery guy,
still brought my letter.
Garbage-collector,
still took away my stinking rubbish.,
And the
cable-guy,
TV-announcer,
Internet technician,
still made me watch the world dying,
searching for a cure.
I would go on and on,
I shouldn't, know for sure
that the least among us,
are,
in fact,
the more useful.
And they count, in life or death,
they remain faithful.

9. Courage to Say "No"

The lack of courage to say "No"
It is such rare in our times
It is responsible for many deaths
It has led to many aborted dreams!

The lack of courage to say "No"
Has sold many ideas to the gallows
Has welcomed many to their early graves
Has forced many to give up their visions!

The courage to say "No"
Is responsible for great inventions
Is the DNA that champions are made of
Is the blood that runs in the veins of
martyrs!

The courage to say "No"
Makes smart women run away from abusers
Makes wise men avoid endangering families
Makes many survive Covid-19 and other
diseases!

Many people are in trouble because they
said, "Yes!"
Many souls are dying because they refused to
say, "No!"
Weak minds easily say "Yes,"
But strong hearts have learned to also say,

"No!"

Stop saying "Yes" to everything
Only say, "Yes", if it is beneficial to you
Do say "No" to nothing,
If it enslaves you to another anew.

10.   It'd Be Well, I

The world may look, sound and feel sad.
It seems there is everywhere bad news.
But remember that
He who has begun a good work in you,
Shall not be derailed by the pandemic.
Don't live like those who don't have hope.
Remember: "The LORD is close
To the broken-hearted
And saves those who are crushed in spirit"
Trust also in the Lord, and He shall provide
your food:
"The LORD does not let the righteous go
hungry..."
During this trying time,
God will not forsake you:
"I was young and now I am old,
Yet I have never seen the righteous forsaken
Or their children begging bread."
You may be alone at home,
But you're not lonely,
Because Jesus is there with you:
"I am with you always, even to the end of
the age."

11.   It'd Be Well, II

Even if you may develop Covid-19
symptoms,
Don't be afraid, for "God is our refuge and
strength,
A very present help in trouble."
And when you're overwhelmed by this
pandemic
And don't know what to do,
Pray, call to your loving God:
"In my distress I called upon the Lord,
And cried out to my God;
He heard my voice from His temple,
And my cry came before Him, even to His
ears."
And last, God is reminding you, that,
"Tell the righteous it will be well with
them..."
And so, shall it be.

12. Cancelled

Everything that is not essential is cancelled.
This includes education attended in person.
Canceled also is prestigious professional
games.
Planes which ace the skies, travel, is
cancelled.

Nothing that is of essence should be
cancelled.
The police. Nurses. Doctors. All healthcare
staffs.
Those whose it is their business to save lives
—
Grocery stores, gas stations are not
cancelled.

After days, hair is over-grown, sagging the
head.
The crass, the messy, and an undergrowth
beard.
Ladies nails cry for a last paint, or they are
dead.
Many saloons and barbershops beg to be
heard.

Look, the monetary indexes are terribly
down.
Dow Industrial breaks many hearts of the
rich.
Empty, is every financial bastion downtown.
Many can't flaunt, can't frolic on the beach.

What's not canceled is home, family, and
love.
Even religious, spiritual centers are
cancelled.
Luxuries. Business. Courts. Taverns.
Suspended.
If contact is not cancelled, life could be
ended.

13.   Politicians as Leaders

Why do we still make politicians leaders?
They have no clues to complex problems
They don't answer questions, they dodge
When they are called to provide statements,
Nay, they spill eulogies and anecdotes
They're shameless, they meander throughout
For a simple "No" or "Yes", they spin into
mazes
As far as they are concerned,
They cause nothing,
They're responsible for nothing,
They didn't do anything
And as for the difficulties at hand,
They only inherited everything.
People everywhere are dying,
Politicians are living,
Everyone is poor and in need,
Politicians are full and flowing
They lead from behind; they sleep in
Parliament
They run departments they can't define
They read speeches they did not write
And they are hired without any qualification.
They have one certification,
They are not afraid, to lie -
Only the truth, shall bid Covid bye!

14.   Easter Poem

I
The Covid-19 pandemic is all about a
disease, a virus
And this just reminds us of the story of our
Lord Jesus
His birth, the first wonder of the world, a
virgin conception
Herod, trying to kill the Baby, his plan
hinged a deception.

II
He grew up normal, like any other child,
physically strong
But unlike any other human being, He did
nothing wrong
At the age of twelve, He confounded the
teachers of law
They tried to dissuade young Jesus, but
found no flaw.

III

As He grew up, everything about Him coiled
in contrasts
Though He was God, He was also human's
special class
And the greatest of these, was the exchanges
He made
Though divine, He became mortal, what a
price He paid.

IV

Through miracles, He changed the order of
entire nature
By parables, He spoke to the intricacy of
man, His creature
But through a painful death, He opened a
new vista of life
And betrothed Himself to His Church, His
body and wife.

V

It is Easter, I want to tell a remorseful, but
blissful story
How humility and wounds paved a daggered
way to glory
In Israel, the highest of criminality was
meted at a cross
It was basest condemnation, lower than
ordure, a curse.

VI

The cross, was the sign that you were not at
all wanted
You were heavenly waste, and earthly dung,
haunted
Hanging there, your crimes, in pain, you
bore as trash
In death, devalued, you became lower than
rubbish.

VII

How can it be that God, the Father, should
subject His Son,
The sinless One, paraded naked, on a tree, in
bright sun?
How could a real criminal, a sinner, me and
you, go free,
But His beloved didn't allow Him from this
cruelty to flee?

VIII

Oh love, kindness, mercy, justice He made
Him to meet
Nailing Him on a tree, sparing not His palms
nor His feet
Ignoring His voice, He did not hear His
solitary prayer
Only anguish, merciless anguish, His dignity
left bare.

IX
Then to our benefit, God His righteousness
to us credited
His position in the sight of men, to His
shame debited
He took all our sins, past, present and future
in His body
His flesh became a large sore, His Word was
our antibody.

X
In His wounds, injuries, lesions, cuts,
blisters, His life gashed
By the stripes, strips, streaks, lines, all
sickness got punished
The scourging plague and infirmity
exchanged for wholeness
The torment, terror and setback imputed to
us as a bonus.

XI
Then the final blow – death – inflicted on
Him enroute to Hell
With His own blood, the price, He freed
captives from the cell
Proclaimed, "Man is whole, cured, healthy,
restored, saved,"
God, to earth and Hades His Son sent, for
man He loved.

XII
Oh Covid, you have no power, the worm's itch is quashed
For He is risen from the abyss, His blood their sins washed
Oh death, oh grave, Satan, by His life your sting is crushed
Those in Him believe, forever their pain, gloom is hushed.

15.   Covid War

The nations are at war, not against each
other
This is not a battle between brother and
brother
There are no flash philosophies, no
ideologies
There are no apologies, and no mythologies.

The cure is not medical, no antibiotics,
either
There is only a social remedy, weapons,
neither
The Generals, presidents need no legal
authority
The enemy is biological combat, in its full
purity.

Over forty million people died in First
World War
Second World War, had seventy-five million
tore
In First, the trigger was a political
assassination
In Second, League's failure, economic
frustration.

Then, only massacres, mass-bombings, genocide,
Now, only disease, starvation, and broken pride
In this war, there're no military ranks, no uniforms
In this war, civilians do chase and weather storms.

This isn't a typical war; it has no engagement rules
It respects neither the fighting wise nor fools
Only distances – social, moral, and even spirituals
No need for armaments, armored cars or warrigals.

The enemy is invisible – hangs on and to everything
So long as it is visible, to it, this foe will cling
Fear – is its foremost malice, with it, it braces
Tear – has broken rank and cursēd men's faces.

Death is common, it is no longer breaking
news
Faith is eroding, people's hope now lies in
booze
Money – is no longer a god; oil has been
debased
Honey is no longer sweet, isolation is the
new taste.

But one flaw this adversary has, it can't rout
unity
If nations, governments bond, bug has no
munity.

16.   The World in
Mourning, First Wave

The sooner the sun rises and sets,
someone has died.
Like vapor they go,
with or without having goodbyed.
There's no funeral home,
no morgue to contain them
There's yelling for grandpa,
for little Moses, it's a shame
There's no crowd to escort
the coronaviroid departed
Only statistics, more news, more bad news,
for the parted
In USA,
they mourned six thousand people today
In Italy,
thirteen thousand people who passed away
Spain lost ten thousand loved ones,
and more counting
While Germany had one thousand plus,
discounting,
In China,
three thousand and more left the earth
In France,
over five thousand couldn't keep life's faith,
They lie without breath about three
thousand in Iran
UK's over-two-thousand bodies

are over and done
And Belgian and Netherlands,
lost over two thousand
Canada, Indonesia,
they put over three-seventy in sand
Close to twenty have died in Africa,
I fear more is to come
Oh, Mother, don't keep silent, let no-one
say, "Be calm!"
For the world is in mourning,
and none is there to soothe.
Oh, no, this pain is gross,
it's worse than extracted tooth.

17.   Second Wave, I

It is here, it has been here, it's not going
The Corona Virus, numbers are growing.
By end May, nations had gone in lockdowns
Shutting counties, many small and large
towns.
Some countries guarded well, including
China
Whiles others the damage wasn't all too
minor.
Many people, the aging, have succumbed
Though some, having to live with it, have
numbed.
The tow on human mind is in millions,
But the blow on economies, in billions.

18.   Second Wave, II

To USA, India, Russia, and Brazil,
It has bequeathed an awful lethal kill.
The nations with female leaders did well,
But those with radical dolts didn't excel.
Africa, except to the South, was spared
Mostly due to strict warnings quickly aired.
Adults and young did not go visiting,
The worker did not do soliciting.
There were restrictions in many a place
And it didn't matter people's class or race.

19.   Second Wave, III

Then did begin Trump to thump the trumpet
When he saw his votes begin to plummet.
He and like others forced the re-opening
Before long, the virus had broken in.
The second wave was finally around,
This period, to run everything aground.
The fear of second closure ran amok
And mask mandates began to be in tuck.
The GOP is breaking social distance rules
As millions get ill at rallies and schools.

20.   Second Wave, IV

This wave two is dangerously stronger
Many European states get it wronger,
The end seems far away in a distance
With no vaccine, there's threat to existence.
This menace loves and behaves like a flu
So, in Winter and Fall it will accrue.
The goal should be to stop the pandemic,
To reduce its spread, making it less endemic.
To that end, wash hands clean, and stay
away;
Do listen to science, wear masks, start today.

21.   Dr. Fauci

You may call him anything, US physician
He is nimble, pure, and a true guardian
He will not bulge to theories of ricardian
Nor move an inch to give up his position.

The barrage of political pressure
Underneath the Trump administration;
He's relentless to save the population
From Coronavirus, that wicked thresher.

For very well he knows, life continues
Even when Trump is clearly defeated
So, he stays, till his mission's completed
His foe won't tire him even with bad news.

Oh, Covid, brag not you slew America
But for the foolishness of its leader
And the greed of the misinformed reader;
They endorse the ideals of Amerika.

Oh, let Fauci lead the way, all the way
Till the shot that'll kill Coronavirus fires
And many a crooked politician retires,
Till life yields to normal, and all is okay.

22.   They Gather

They gather, in masses, in rallies
As many a death and fatality tallies
They wear no masks, the majority
And those protected, are a minority.
They chant, "Maga," as coffins pie
And repeat slogans, as elderlies die.
Oh, this ruthless public murder,
In their president, they've no girder.
Oh, this total reckless disregard,
The Great Nation, has no guard.
They hug and part, like normal times
No distancing, youth die en primes.

23. Western Virus

The thoroughfare that treks to Covidland
Is plagued by a long, meandering garland.
And silhouettes of broken effigies
Do hang in gory on smitten elegies.
It is the Western Virus, Gravorous,
A descendant of the arbovirus.
Anathemia laments deliriously,
As bell tolls Invocacio, serially.
The venom of AIDS conquered, barely,
And mighty Influenza A, lived, rarely.
The deep hand of disease rigged Africa,
But Covid found a home in America.
The rich, brave have him, so do the stars,
He shuts life, is limitless, worse than SARS.

24.   To Lock or Not to Lock

A raid of deadly bugs, the world in shambles
To lock or not to lock, the earth gambles;
Nanas are dying and so are young ones,
Every day, daughters are infected, so are
sons;
But selfish politicians refuse to accept fate
Their own interests they parade but not of
state;
Morgues are inundated, hospitals are
overflowing,
And there is no space to lay bodies,
overthrowing;
Oh, America, Europe, Africa, and even Asia,
There is much grief inside Eurasia.
No time in history saw an ingesting of bad
news,
Everywhere people wake up but with blues;
The enemy, so small, and yet so powerful,
It's sting, so invisible, and yet so hurtful.
Armies of men, fight, mask, by all means
possible;
Do stay, find vaccine, make it not
transposable.

25. Lamebration

This global winter of discontent's ended,
Oh, may the world celebrate and lament
This lamebration should to our victory sage
For it is not the might, but the proud fall;
The wise in their own understanding,
Who, thicken to moral reason by wealth,
Had forgotten their own nation's health
And corrupted religion with hefty orations.
The Trump has miambly fallen to delirium
Whence Omaha, hundreds left in frozen
cold,
Oh, lamebration, then came the vote day,
And they watch a democratic dictator drop.
Oh, Covid, president's pride you do chop!

26.   The Variant

At the epicenter of a vaccine
Then dawns an era of a new variant
It was neither expected nor foreseen
Alas, human freedom is still on hunt.

Oh, Covid, unable to contain you,
Oh, calendar on-end, nothing but death
Only grief, devastations into truth
Oh, nations do suffocate on short breath.

Such is the state of affairs, sketch a dirge,
Sounds of delight have ended, hazily
Seasons of passing only wisdom purge,
Surely, minds have of late veered crazily.

There is a new variation, deadly fast
It locks down cities, economies fold
No tango, no music, none is to last,
But to terrific hope we rush to wold.

27.   Breaking Point

There are no available beds to sick
The sick are told to go home and die
The dead have no morgue to be rested
And the resting place has no-one to dig.
It is "patients dying like flies."
Giftshops, chapels, are turned into hospitals
Unimaginable is an understatement,
The pick has reached one thousand percent,
And there is nowhere ambulances can go.
Oh, America, Oh, South Africa, O world,
What really, truly went wrong?
Why don't we call it, "War-time medicine"?
Unsustainable, what made it jettison?

28. Battle on Winds

So, I look up daily from my southern window
And all seems fine, no notable innuendo
Serve for the blowing winds, and falling snow,
The roads are still busy, gentle airs still blow.

A battle on winds
Strong cells it grinds
Only death it minds
Life's rare, it finds.

Till I make pause and hear non-breaking news
There's nothing extraordinary, except the blues.
The bulb flickers steadily, but it isn't the light
Eyes can see, but it doesn't look like sight.

A battle on winds
Strong cells it grinds
Only death it minds
Life's rare, it finds.

One out of five has the deadly coronavirus,
And that could be your next neighbor,
Cyrus;
One out of hundred morgues have dead
souls
With no angels meeting them on the shoals.

A battle on winds
Strong cells it grinds
Only death it minds
Life's rare, it finds.

Irrelevant, irrelevant, are all nations'
artilleries
Then comes a message of hope from
heavens,
"Wear a mask, socially distance, stay home,"
There's no room to wonder, no place to
roam.

A battle on winds
Strong cells it grinds
Only death it minds
Life's rare, it finds.

29.　Ode to Hope

You come out with force, swinging,
You have all bells forcibly ringing.
You mean to silence the human race,
You devastate its progeny in every place.

You lock them up, decimate their lives
Husbands, you make rude to their wives
Children, for sure, you deny them play,
And all churches meet on Zoom to pray.

Streets are empty, there's no joyful noise
Your lethal pulse, planned fates it destroys
Uncovered, you pounce like a rogue missile,
You turn to gory; you murder open smiles.

Faces cannot be wide, can't be beautiful
Whitened teeth are hidden, can't be dutiful
Fear, with it, you have made a solid pact
Whoever dances, against him you act.

Death, Oh, death, and more of it, reported
What was straight, simple, is now distorted
Friends and lovers, left pale, frustrated
Minds that thought, left blank, contorted.

There is sadness, in old people's homes
Hair on heads, no grooming, retired combs
Burial is fast, no-one dares to say goodbye
Sanitoriums are now where people go to die.

You are ruthless, worse than The Grinch
You have no mercy, and you don't flinch
When you attack, you're silent, like a serpent
When you prick, you're like honed perpent.

You drink blood, you vomit drops of venom
Your export, people buy it like denim
You respect no bonds of friendships
Only with death, you kiln partnerships.

You've changed the order of commerce
Traders and vendors can't make promises
The rich, are as the poor, both can't move
If they do, them from the earth, you remove.

Radios and TVs, now sell death as news
Employers to employees, have no excuse
Governments have embraced Socialism
No-one hides anymore into their catechism.

But you've forgotten one central thing,
That hope is here, it is now, it is king.
Hope is planning your downfall, Covid,
You will fall flat, you'll remember Ovid.

Hope is mobilizing a cure, to slice you open
To swallow you whole like a gaping ocean
To render you victimless, that's your fear
You will not laugh, you will not again, jeer.

Hope has built a small camp by each city
To shame you with testings, what a pity,
You will never again kill us without data
You'll not reduce us to zombies for dagga.

Hope has insight into you, we now know
you
So far, what we don't know of you, is so few
You may morph into some native variants,
But we'll get you and render you inglorious.

You're not smart, Covid, not like our
scientists
They've lined up vaccines, with superb
finalist
Soon, our politicians will also get smarter
And will distribute it to all, faster, harder.

Then, who shall have the last and loud laugh,
Who will speak and advocate on your
behalf?
You will try to come back in another form,
I warn you; we'll raise against you a
hailstorm.

You have bragged, that so far, you've won,
And that you're going strong, you're not
done.
We admit, but don't think we are naive,
But know that we will not forever bereave.

Hope is building a new agenda for us all,
It's so large, it's being called a "Laugh Mall,"
We shall meet our friends again, dance again,
And our old normalcy, we shall surely gain.

Boys and girls will meet in old playgrounds,
They will ride their bikes, frolic
undergrounds,
They'll toboggan, play *chiyenga*, and dream,
With bliss, at their lungs' tops, they'll scream.

Hope would have won, again, mighty hope
Only you have the power to make us cope,
To provide us with hooves with which to
gallop
To life, you hold us, like a stamped
envelope.

30.   Fear

It coils wriggly across front and back
It has hit Toronto and Peel regions hard
America, has passed over five hundred
And the number is in thousands, no less.
It's snake-like movement is in shadows
As it spreads fear among old, the young;
A cough, is no longer just a common flu
A fever, not a symptom of Nile Fever,
Both shortness of breath and vomiting,
May just be the avenue it takes to kill.
A mask can break its forward motion,
But it can't prevent its lethal penetration;
The human affair has turned into a hell,
And a vaccine injection is just on its way.

31.   As a Prayer

Lord, my Father who is in Heaven
I pray, first, for the world in trouble.
For those infected with Covid-19,
And for those who are affected by it.

I pray, a vaccine be a panacea, leaven
To rekindle people's health in double,
So that the ravages of this Covid-19,
Won't be egregiously felt even a bit.

That it will not the elderly threaten
I pray, send its venom to the rubble
That the world will not fear Covid-19,
Nor to its enslaving power, submit.

Reprieve, I pray, us from this leaden
Give us courage, our effort, redouble.
Break the menace that be Covid-19,
And long and good life for all, permit.

As we prepare for Covid-Armageddon
Oh, Lord, don't render us into stubble.
A victory we must win over Covid-19,
Our fight for normalcy we shan't quit.

32.　　　February 24th, 2021

One died of the virus in Bhutan
And nine perished there in Taiwan
Fourteen died in Antigua and Barbuda
Over twenty-one thousand in Canada.

Close to fifty thousand died in South Africa;
God, spared death to the people of
Dominica,
And the saints of the enclaved State of Holy
See
Even as He did spare the nation of Timor-
Leste.

It is close to two hundred thousand in
Mexico
While about eight thousand deaths in
Morocco
But over three thousand died in Armenia
Yet, thankfully, none did in New Caledonia.

The inhabitants of Macao, Laos nations
And Saint Kitts & Nevis's populations,
Neither Greenland nor Saint Pierre &
Miquelon,
Had any soul going to Hell or to Heaven.

Over six thousand in Guatemala
But none did do perish in Anguilla
They have no Covid death in Falkland
Islands
So do they have none in Solomon Islands.

Still more than a thousand in Albania,
Only twenty-one in Covid-rejecting
Tanzania
Over thirty-five-thousand in Indonesia
But zero deaths were reported in Micronesia.

God, have mercy on the United States,
For it leads the globe in deaths, state by
states;
India is number two, while Brazil ranks
third,
Russia is fourth, UK ranked fifth in the
world.

33.   A Disease Unlike Covid

It shall be a year of mourning unlike any
It shall paralyze commerce and kill many
From the lands surrounded by great waters,
With crimson floods filled with slaughters,
Yet, not as spoils of war, only tiny missiles,
With viral efficiency in their deathly thistles.

No physician will be spared, no mastery
For long, no vaccine will be satisfactory.
The open world shall be the most secret
And confined spaces, its fatal weakest;
The sick would wish for death as sweets
The healthy will pent of anguish in streets.

There is no sectorial beneficiary, all victims
Order shall turn to mischief, no systems.
Nothing but hope, and a lad, shall remedy,
But its sting, shall never erase the memory.
The qualms against Covid shall not be heard,
And its miseries shall never again be
inferred.

INDEX

CHARLES MWEWA

Charles Mwewa (LLM – cand.) is a prolific author, poet, political thinker, and Christian and community leader. Mwewa has written no less than 30 books and counting. Mwewa and his wife, Clarice, and their three daughters, Emmerance, Tashany-Idyllia, and Cuteravive, reside in the Canadian Capital City of Ottawa.

AUTHOR'S CONTACT

Email Address: charlesmwewa@gmail.com

Phone Number: 1-647-458-7435

Facebook: facebook.com/charlesmwewa

Twitter: twitter.com/charlesmwewa

Author's Website: www.charlesmwewa.com